Let's go by Plane

Barbara Hunter

Heinemann
LIBRARY

Little Nippers

www.heinemann.co.uk/library
Visit our website to find out more information about **Heinemann Library** books.

To order:
☎ Phone 44 (0) 1865 888066
▤ Send a fax to 44 (0) 1865 314091
▣ Visit the Heinemann Bookshop at www.heinemann.co.uk/library to browse our catalogue and order online.

First published in Great Britain by Heinemann Library, Halley Court, Jordan Hill, Oxford OX2 8EJ, part of Harcourt Education. Heinemann is a registered trademark of Harcourt Education Ltd.

Editorial: Jilly Attwood and Claire Throp
Design: Jo Hinton-Malivoire and bigtop, Bicester, UK
Models made by: Jo Brooker
Picture Research: Lodestone Publishing Limited
Production: Lorraine Warner

Originated by Dot Gradations
Printed and bound in China by South China Printing Company

ISBN 0 431 16464 9 (hardback)
06 05 04 03 02
10 9 8 7 6 5 4 3 2 1

ISBN 0 431 16469 X (paperback)
06 05 04 03 02
10 9 8 7 6 5 4 3 2 1

British Library Cataloguing in Publication Data
Hunter, Barbara
Let's go by plane
387.7'42
A full catalogue record for this book is available from the British Library.

Acknowledgements
The publishers would like to thank the following for permission to reproduce photographs:
Alvey and Towers pp. **10**, **11**; Bubbles p. **8** (Peter Sylent); Collections p. **9a** (Chris Honeywell); Quadrant Picture Library p. **4-5**, pp. **7**, **16** (E. de Malglaive), p. **14** (Simon Everett), p. **15**, p. **18-19** (Jeremy Hoare), p. **20-21** (Mark Wagner); Sally and Richard Greenhill p. **6**, **13**, p. **17** (Richard Greenhill); Tografox p. **9b** (R. D. Battersby); Travel Ink p. **12** (Brian Hoffman).

Cover photograph reproduced with permission of Quadrant: The Flight Collection.

The publishers would like to thank Annie Davy for her assistance in the preparation of this book.

Every effort has been made to contact copyright holders of any material reproduced in this book. Any omissions will be rectified in subsequent printings if notice is given to the publishers.

Contents

Journeys

Many people go by plane. They are called passengers.

BIG planes can take more than 500 passengers!

Why do people go by plane?

Holiday

Tickets

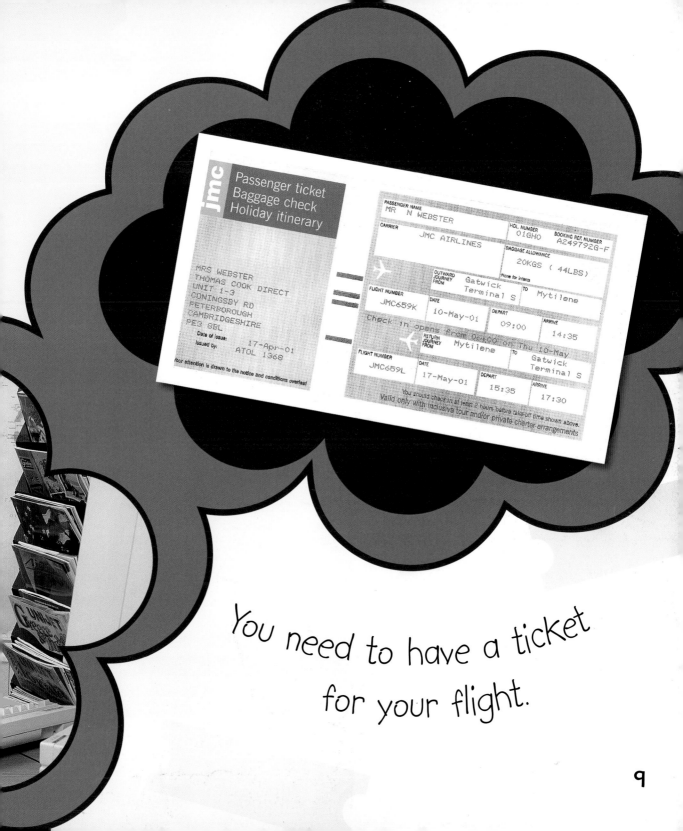

You need to have a ticket
for your flight.

At the airport

You show your ticket and passport at the check-in desk.

You put your heavy luggage
on a conveyor belt.

In the departure lounge

You wait for your flight in the departure lounge.

Then you board
the plane.

When the pilot is ready the plane **zooms** along the runway.

Meal time

Air stewards give you
a meal to eat.

Yummy yum!

Bing bong!

If you would like a drink you can ring the bell.

Movie time

Some journeys by plane take a very **long** time so there are films to watch.

Must For Playing.

When the plane arrives you have to wait for your luggage to be unloaded.

The luggage goes round and round a conveyor belt.

Shapes

What shapes can you see on a plane journey?

tail

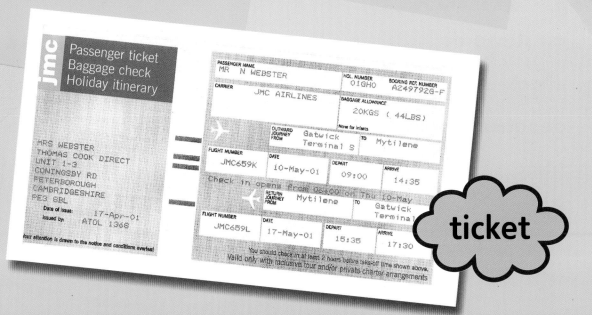

ticket

wheel

Index

The end

Notes for adults

This series supports the young child's knowledge and understanding of their world and, in particular, their mathematical development. Mathematical language like *heavy/light, long/short,* and an introduction to different shapes and positional vocabulary such as *near/far,* make this series useful in developing mathematical skills. The following Early Learning Goals are relevant to the series:
• find out about, and identify, some features of living things, objects and events that they observe
• show an awareness of similarities in shapes in the environment
• observe and use positional language.

The series explores journeys and shows four different ways of travelling and so provides opportunities to compare and contrast them. Some of the words that may be new to them in **Let's Go By Plane** are *aeroplane, passengers, check-in, luggage, passport, departure, arrival, board, runway* and *steward/stewardess.* Since words are used in context in the book this should enable the young child to gradually incorporate them into their own vocabulary.

The following additional information about plane journeys may be of interest: Most plane journeys cover long distances but in a relatively short length of time. Most planes have a logo on their tail indicating the airline company that fly the plane. There are many different types of planes including the very fast Concorde.

Follow-up activities
The child could collect pictures of different planes and suggest who might be travelling on them and why. Children who have been on a plane may enjoy making a record of their journey by drawing, writing or tape recording their experiences to share with others.